Get Me Out of Here

GET ME OUT OF HERE

SACHIKO MURAKAMI

Talonbooks

Talonbooks
278 East First Avenue, Vancouver, British Columbia, Canada V5T 1A6
www.talonbooks.com

First printing: 2015

Typeset in Albertan
Printed and bound in Canada on 100% post-consumer recycled paper

Cover design by Brian Houle
Interior design by Typesmith

Talonbooks gratefully acknowledges the financial support of the Canada Council for the Arts, the Government of Canada through the Canada Book Fund, and the Province of British Columbia through the British Columbia Arts Council and the Book Publishing Tax Credit.

Library and Archives Canada Cataloguing in Publication

Murakami, Sachiko, 1980–, author
　　　Get me out of here / Sachiko Murakami.

Poems.
ISBN 978-0-88922-925-9 (pbk.)

　　　I. Title.

PS8626.U72G48 2015　　　C811'.6　　　C2014-907071-3

For Kimiko and Judah Murakami

- concrete poetry
↳ poems. become small
visual factors.

CONTENTS

DEPARTURES

Fatima uses power tools, buffs leather while speaking Arabic into a cellphone tucked into her djellaba.

Elee Kraljii Gardiner, **YVR**-YYZ-BOS

1.

Fatima joins me in the life-sized corridor.

Our vantage makes the most of geometry.

We see every exit.

She pulls the last of the boarding passes from my pockets.

My departure, meaningless.

We hold each other's gaze, shyly.

We will wait until the shift is over.

Hands pressed to tiled wall, its held chill a respite from recycled air.

It's like we're real, here.

"Almost," we whisper. But not quite.

I reposition glass walls, play planner, mock door.

The strangers hurry in as they always do in situations like these.

They line up to have their faces buffed to plainness.

They are always lining up. ← like the words in a book that she later defies

3

2.

Fatima wakes in a non-place where her name means less than the enormity.

Atima, says she. At times, I'm an item.

Item: Sachiko.

Stump of a gal in an imaginary airport.

Feet stamped to bring feeling back.

Who ignored the sensation of being watched and focused on leaving.

Try again. Look up. Feet on the ground.

(Name three things you see.)

3.

Fatima and I take a breather from the unreal.

She flips back to deftly polish.

She leaves for her break through a door I can't enter.

In the real world I am useless.

(Three things again. Don't look up.)

The sound of Fatima's djellaba as she walks away.

Rustle, rustle. *Rustle, rustle?*

Did you hear that?

Did you?

Walking into the terminal, early-morning flight — and I feel right at home.

Christopher Schaberg, **MSY**–EWR–BOS

Did you pre-watch the video demos of the proper use of the self check-in terminals.

Did you practice the brief, unburdened walk through the security gate. Your sweet-spot gait.

Did you anticipate where the shadows would be. How your fingers wouldn't reach.

Are you prepared for any eventuality with regard to your shoes.

The glacé-lifted air, the precise light. Its filigree tinkle on your fingers.

No, none of it happens with your eyes open.

You have Kristoff's latte, carry what was meant for him.

The white of the cup so like the white of all the other cups.

You step again into the terminal and your particles drift.

The glass-filtered light, the precise air, etc.

Filigree thinginess meant for the paying passengers.

The self check-in spits its ribboning, gushing tickets.

Your carry around what was meant for you.

You drink without incident the shitty, familiar coffee.

A four-year-old boy was running to catch up with his older sister and he followed her out onto the moving sidewalk and, two paces in, he froze into a low crouch, wobbling, arms out, watching her get away.

Laurie D. Graham, YYZ-YEG

he who senses the world's shift

        would unfurl to nearly flying if he would

    relax into gravity's   loosening

        but we are not birds

who are   released from

    the ground by their wings

    while mine   keep me tethered

to some   other   time

    not quite nor ever

here

where the world   changes

    when the echo   comes   unexpected in

a sigh escaping a body barely   aware it is

    twisted inward to   protect a mind from a

moment

    and its flight

I saw a flock of gleeful, shrieking almost-teenagers running in search of a washroom, when one long-limbed girl broke ahead, located the women's side, and then quickly rejoined the group, screeching with her friends that she didn't know where the washrooms were, either.

Kimiko Murakami, **YVR**–YYZ

The flock knows
to twist its corpus east
and west, no reason
but the wind
and one rule:
when your neighbour moves,
so do you move
with the delight
of being lost together:
a noisy sangha
taking refuge in the descant
that cuts into wordless thrum:
we are here, we are here,

we are here

we are here

here we are

are we here

wear her here

weigh her ear

wear her air

hear her air

weigh her air

weigh air here

we are her

are we her

we are here we are here we are here we are here we are here we   we are here we are here we are
        here we are here we are   we are here we are here   we
are here we are here we are   we are here we are here we are   we are here   are here
we are here we are here we are here we are here we are here we are here we   we are here we are
here we are here we are here we are here we are here we   here we are here we   here we
are here we are   here we are here we   here we are here we   are here we are
        we are here we are here we are here we are here   are here we are here we   here we are
here we are here we are here we are here we are here we are here
here we are here we are   we are here we are here we are   we are here we

                we are here
              we are here we are
            here we are here we are
          here we are here we
        are here we are
        here we are here we are
        here we are here we are here
        we are here we are here we are here
         we are here we are here we are here we
          are here we are here we are here we are here
          we are here we are here we are here we are
            here we are here we are here we are here
              we are here we are here we are here
                we are here we are here we are here we are
              here we are here we are here we are here we
            are here we are here we are here we
            are here we are here we are here
             we are here we are here we are here we are
             here we are here we are here we are here we are
             here we are here we are here we are here we
               are here we are here we are here we are
               here we are here we are here we are
                here we are here we are here we
                  are here we are here we are
                    here we are here
                    we are here
                    we are

we are here we are here we are here we are here we are here we are here we are here we are here we are
here we are here we are here we are here we are here we are here we are here we are here we are here we
are here we are here we are here we are here we are here we are here we are here

For female voices. A vocalized murmuration as incantation, as game: we are here.

FIRST
Participants assemble in a cluster with score. Vocal level is "murmur." Voices choose any of the lines in any order, at any pace. Continues until all participants feel they are familiar with the lines, at least two minutes. Effect is a soft, indecipherable uttering. One voice takes a sharp in-breath to indicate the movement to SECOND. Voice continues taking sharp, audible in-breath until everyone notices and ceases. Participants may discard score.

Pause

SECOND
Participants break into small groups of two or three. Vocal level is "above murmur." Style is call-and-response. Participants listen to their partner's line, then respond with a different line, and so on. One voice takes a sharp in-breath to indicate the movement to THIRD.

Pause

THIRD
One groups joins with another. Vocal level is "voiced," charged with the energy of the growing group. Participants continue call-and-response, passing it between participants in whatever order seems organic, using whatever gestures arise organically (caller may point at the responder, or "clap" the "tag" to the responder, or hold the hand of the responder, or make eye contact with the responder, etc.). By now it is a game of vocal hacky sack. One voice takes a sharp in-breath to indicate the movement to LAST.

Pause

LAST
Participants form a circle if they have not yet. They chant, "we are here / are we here / here we are," growing louder or softer as the group's consciousness dictates. When at full volume, one member inhales, sharply, repeatedly until noticed, to indicate the movement to RELEASE.

Pause

RELEASE
All participants take one deep-voiced in-breath, hold, and release voiced out-breath "her" to the circle.

The burly security guard hands a tissue to the girl sniffing back tears and says, "My dear, take this."

Kaarina Mikalson, **YWG**–YHZ

My dear, take this face leaking self, take this
small token of my business, *but if you're asking*
for my advice, crying isn't going to get you
any sympathy around here at the crossing
from in here to out there you will need to take
it easy on the sympathetic *looks*
like you can take it with you (you can't take it with you)
out of your bag, please. Is this your
glance through glass (farther than tarmac,
past the field, the cemetery) – remove self from situation
to keep self *in as it comes* (it will come, in waves,
amid cloud, your heart racing behind)
(his heart racing behind)
(heart racing behind)

Essential read as Sentinel.

Christine McNair, **YOW**–YYZ

LATENESS I READ AS LEANEST IS READ AS EASEL TINS READ AS LATES SIN READ AS TEASES NIL READ AS ALIEN SETS READ AS AISLE NEST READ AS LASSIE NET READ AS ANISE LEST READ AS ALE STEINS READ AS ELAN SITES READ AS SALE INSET READ AS SANE ISLET READ AS SANEST LIE READ AS NEAT ISLES READ AS SEA SILENT READ AS EAST LINES READ AS ASSET LINE READ AS SAIL TENSE READ AS A LIT SENSE READ AS SAINT ELSE READ AS SANS ELITE READ AS A SLEET SIN READ AS A SEEN LIST READ AS SENSE ALIT READ AS A SITE LENS READ AS ALE SETS IN READ AS ALE SET SIN READ AS ELAN SETS I READ AS LEAN SETS I READ AS LEAN SET IS READ AS LANES SET I READ AS SALE SENT I READ AS SALE SET IN READ AS SEAL SENT I READ AS SANE LEST I READ AS SANEST ELI READ AS ANTELESS I READ AS SEA ENLIST READ AS SEAS LET IN READ AS TEALESS IN READ AS EAT LESS IN READ AS ALI TENSES READ AS SLANT I SEE READ AS LAST SEE IN READ AS AS NESTLE I READ AS AS STEEL IN READ AS AS SEEN LIT READ AS AS LIES NET READ AS AS LINE SET READ AS AS SINE LET READ AS AS ELEN ITS READ AS AT LESSEN I READ

No punctuation

anagram.

Tripping on tarmac heels adjunct, prop plane stutters and luggage trucks the distance.

Christine McNair, **BDL-YUL**

, plane trucks distance heels stutters tarmac on prop adjunct and luggage tripping the distance, stutters on and plane adjunct luggage tripping trucks tarmac heels the prop adjunct distance the stutters plane trucks and tarmac tripping, prop luggage heels on distance tripping trucks plane prop and, tarmac adjunct stutters heels the luggage on tripping, plane tarmac trucks luggage stutters on and prop adjunct distance the heels heels prop on trucks, adjunct tarmac distance and the luggage tripping plane stutters tripping, and prop heels adjunct tarmac distance the on plane stutters trucks luggage , heels prop and tripping luggage tarmac stutters plane adjunct the on trucks distance prop tripping adjunct luggage and heels trucks stutters distance on tarmac the, plane distance heels adjunct plane tarmac luggage trucks and, stutters prop the on tripping stutters, tarmac adjunct prop and distance on the heels tripping plane trucks luggage stutters heels tarmac distance and plane adjunct luggage tripping on the trucks prop, tarmac plane prop on, and trucks heels stutters the adjunct tripping distance luggage stutters and distance prop tarmac heels the tripping, on trucks luggage plane adjunct adjunct on stutters trucks plane the tarmac and, prop distance heels luggage tripping *[handwritten: to spell (spanks)]*

Canadian domestic: Bodyskin sets off no alarms at security checkpoint.

[handwritten: ↳ easy to conceal]

Sonnet L'Abbé, YVR–YLW

Oxygen, hydrogen, nitrogen, carbon, calcium,
phosphorus a spark in the night, potassium, sulphur to keep hell close,
salt to bring thoughts to blood, chlorine to dissolve the stains.
Magnesium, iron of the hammering heart, fluorine, zinc,
silicon, rubidium, strontium, bromine, lead to fill and copper to case the bullet,
aluminum, cadmium, cerium, barium, a tin can to store rage, iodine, titanium, and boron.
Selenium, nickel, chromium, manganese, arsenic for our enemies' letters,
lithium to slack the mood's pendulum, mercury to gauge its rising heat,

molybdenum, germanium, cobalt to help the blues adhere, antimony,
silver shining with the moon's false light,
niobium, zirconium to call up falsehoods, lanthanum, tellurium,
gallium, yttrium, bismuth, thallium, indium, gold to craft the breastplate,
scandium, tantalum, vanadium, thorium, samarium,
tungsten, beryllium, radium, polonium, uranium to rip open stalemate.

[handwritten, vertical: murder]

Distracted jazz musician, horsehair carry-on in slide-by executive, taste fuel with lungs, then breathe.

Kim Minkus, **ORD**-YVR

Priorities

Dishevelled woman, iPhone frames anywhere, wait for text message, then breathe ·
Youth pastor, hoard power outlet at departure gate, throttle with eyes, then breathe

Barefoot and eastward, prayer mat laid in interfaith space, taste presence with spine, then breathe
Retired mother, jewellery placed in plastic bin, cut diamond with throat, then breathe

Dishevelled self, trace frame of bathroom door with eyes, wait for silence, then breathe
Actually me, hoard power at departure gate, justify with imaginary limp, then breathe
Within the now, look for myself in the crowd until I grow weary, then breathe
Place everything valuable including self in the bin, then breathe

Face of conjured crowd, edge blurred by lazy sight, click tongue at clatter, then breathe
Word labour, dull flint thud on flat stone, scratch sight with Internet, then breathe
Labour face include crowd with self and throat laid, then breathe
Then breathe with labour include self in crowd click tongue at Internet, then breathe

Then return for the painful apprehension again, then breathe
Then return again for painful apprehension, return for apprehension, return, then breathe

This section is closed.

Beatrice Kraljii, **YVR**–YYZ–BOS

If I had a superpower it would be for quick
exits. I drop the curtain, clip the cordon.
Nothing to see here. Keep moving.

If I had a question it would be, what happened to the poem
when I stopped looking for it. I fill each step
with the urgency to move forward. Huff past saunter.

Between the baggage drop and the jet bridge that carries us into flight
I pause to break the knees of every line.
A closed door cracks open by the mimic of movement.

Where does desire go when I keep moving
as though leashed to the future.
When someone else's plane is called.

A warning of the end keeps me rushing to the gate.

Three New Year's Eve travellers cuddle their carry-on doggies.

Sonnet L'Abbé, **YKF**-YYC-YLW

Before the flight's stern retreat from the future,
love clutched to love's resting place.

Will love be ripped away
or will she leave it for dust to veil.

Will she leave. Of course
she will leave.

Not all departures are torn-asunders.
Not all new years are worth mentioning.

Autobiographical pain
is still pain.

Fur damp where she sought
again the certain scent.

Did you have a good time, that night.
How happy were you.

The hipster with the Duck Hunt T-shirt and lip ring could be Eric Bana if he tried.

Jennica Harper, **SFO**-LAX

This face so like the one I saw last week,
askance. I mean, I think. Then I look back down
at my phone. Even now

while I brush at features
place him in the lineup
and call the observers.
"Eric Bana," they won't say.

It's spoiled. They know exactly what he will do with his hands.

I make a mirror face for the glass.
From here I have no idea what I look like.

Re-rearrange our faces — mine for your idea,
yours for the idea of mine.
With this filter we don't
look like ourselves even when we try.

Due to the sprawl, soon the airport will be an urban island <u>akin to Nose Hill</u>,

ryan fitzpatrick, **YYC**–YYZ

From satellite, a numb hole in the urban plan,
or relief from its logic.

All known views shift gaze away;
see how downtown looks like a snow globe!

Come back to the gate.
You're still in this line to get to the next line.

To look inward at the Calgary International Airport,
<u>stretch the idea of</u> plateau, then write down "plateau" in case you forget.

Cut open doors and windows to create a place.
In its absence, there is the function of a place.

Come back to the experience of this uncomfortable chair / of this plateau,
then <u>while live-tweeting this</u>, call it "here."

Google "here." Google Maps "here." Google Images "here."
YouTube "here." <u>Ask your followers</u>, "here?"

[Hint: we're not really "<u>here.</u>"] → Busy on phones ??

19

Airports are 79 percent glass.

Ivar Kraljii, **YVR**-YYZ-BOS

Clever to clad this structure in amorphous solid,
its molecular disorder quenched long ago, and now –
well, that's as far as my physics goes. Eyes, glassy,
drift through solid light toward field.
From here, a dim landscape
far from the clutch of figures
pressing forward, forward.
Somewhere else, where sky rubs
tarmac smooth. Nothing to quantify
the wind or other tumult, no structure
weak enough to blow down before me,
just silence provided by sight, and then
some giant impossible lumbering thing,
distant as an image of a body pressed to glass.

Security has its price: "this area is under surveillance."

Christopher Schaberg, **BOS**–IAH–MSY

A bird is having trouble with the airport floor.

ryan fitzpatrick, **YYZ**-YVR

```
int passengersCheckedIn;
int currentTerminalPassengers;
String prophecy = "The sky is falling";
int experience;
int floor;
int passenger;
boolean skyfalling = false;
boolean floorIntegrity = true;
Serial passengersCheckpoint;

void setup(){
 passengersCheckedIn = passengersCheckpoint.value;
 currentTerminalPassengers = passengersCheckedIn;
}

void draw() {
 if (skyfalling == true) {
  disasterResponse();
 } else if (sky == visible){
  monitor();
 } else {
  checkFloor();
 }
}

void disasterResponse(){
 for (passenger = 0; passenger<currentTerminalPassengers; passenger++)
 {
  express(prophecy);
 }
}

void monitor() {
 if (passengersCheckedIn > currentTerminalPassengers) {
  express(prophecy);
  currentTerminalPassengers++;
 }
}

void checkFloor(){
 if (floorIntegrity != true) {
  skyfalling == true;
 }
}
```

If the sky falls inward and the idea is enough to set a chicken running through the terminal, wings akimbo;

Then the chicken fails with the floor and her prophecy is relinquished;.

Else if the sky stays put and the chicken worries it to prove a point about art;

Then allow the sky to actually crumble;

Else if the sky should destroy the fluidity of experience with its terrible weight;

Then for each vantage create the great disaster;

Else if the crowd is collectively lost in thought;

Then spawn new chicken and run prophecy;

Return results and check again for signal;

chopOffTheChickenHead();

println("just from an idea!");

I'm younger than two-thirds of the flight by about fifty years; so many people needed wheelchairs that the airline ran out, borrowed a complete fleet from a neighbouring airline, and even accommodated a surly elderly couple that admitted they were lying about needing wheelchairs, but since so many other people had secured wheelchairs for themselves, they deserved them too — "it's the principle of the thing."

Angela Szczepaniak, YYZ–LGW

How does a wheelchair fit down the aisle of an aircraft?

How is your construction of what followed relevant to your reading of this poem?

What principle is demonstrated by the surly couple? By the speaker? By the airline? By the poet? Pick two. Compare and contrast.

How does memory fit inside a poem?

What is the speaker doing that the elderly are not doing? What muscles does it involve? How supple are these muscles?

What is the likelihood the speaker observed this from a wheelchair?

What is the significance of the speaker observing a wheelchair caravan on a flight that departed at exactly 00:00 on January 1, 2013?

What time is it now? Now? Now? Now? Now? Now?

What is the difference between an inquiry and a demand, poetry-wise?

Why might the speaker be on a flight on January 1? What is the likelihood of her wearing a festive hat?

How alike or unlike are the flight and the ferry boat that crosses the River Styx?

Are the passengers on the River Styx ferry boat happy, neutral, or sad? What difference would wheelchairs make? Festive hats?

At what rate is the speaker's body declining in comparison to the bodies of the elderly? The poet's body? The reader's? Compare and contrast your body's state from the start of this poem to the end of this line. What might a person do to slow the rate of the body's decline? Show your work.

How can you tell when an anecdote is finished?
How can you tell when this poem?

At the Las Vegas airport you can gamble and smoke while waiting for your plane to board.

David McGimpsey, LAS-YUL

Lost her number, maxed the Visa, left to wait on a stool in the Lucky Streak Lounge.

The flash & pizzazz hangover, insolent buzz, lazy roll of the dice.

The satisfaction that comes with threes.

With looking like a #losersofinstagram.

Welcome almost-home. Then welcome to the path,

and the reason for the journey; or, I like the pings and beeps.

The machine chatty in a tongue I nearly decipher.

Like Dutch but pingier and beepier.

Doorgaan! Doorgaan! Doo—

Lamé set off the beeper at security more than once, was tacitly placed in a carry-on.

Funnel all the noise into one sound. All the movement

into one movement. All drinks into one, ultimate drink.

And another and another and another.

After hearing a man shout "Jim! Jim! JIM!" at another man until he turned around, it dawns on me that
Goatboy is on my flight to Kelowna.

Tanis MacDonald, **YVR**-YLW

It dawns on Jim that Tanis is on his flight to Kelowna. .
The Internet brays, "Tanis! Tanis! TANIS!"

The data double turns around, its form
disassembled into usable, braying metrics.

Google: "account for the humanimal in mid-nineties broadcast comedy."
Google: myaah, myaah, myaah.

Beneath the toque, whose oblivious ears?
Beneath thumbs, whose mouths bray?

I spit into a tube and send away for an account of my genes.
I catch sight of myself in a mirror and inwardly bray.

Kelowna: site of my sister's birth, as captured by the Vital Statistics Agency.
Kelowna: where goats go to revive their careers as content producers.

OMG, @PoetTanis just sat down next to me!
@SachikoMurakami: pics or it didn't happen.

The tiled koi pond is filled with lobsters.

Heather Jessup, **YHZ**–YYC–YVR

Heather, there is no evidence on the Internet to confirm
that this koi pond filled with lobsters actually exists.
Knowing you are not a liar, I can only assume
you are a romantic that misread *holding tank* as
koi pond. The lobsters, not ornament, but there
for *souvenir*: remembrance boiled alive and served
to friends. *I was here.* Recall drips with sweet butter.
Here. I clear the tank of lobsters. What now, a wishing well?
Signs that say you really oughtn't throw coins? Clear the coins,
pull the plug. *Wherever*, intones the PA. The unfilled space
a place to lie down before security comes with its hook, with its hustle.
Race to the gate where the poem takes us into *there*'s air
with your rusty laugh, your old cellphone with its cricketing clitter.
Wherever, wherever, wherever.

Older man sits across from his wife, calls out the weather network: Tokyo, 11; Cancun, 32; London, 8.

Wanda O'Connor, **YUL**–YVR

Gas goes dry. Liners run on sun ship snowbirds to Svalbard, slashed Iqaluit fares.
Snowbirds flock to tundra, seek shelter from summer's endless high noon.
Snowbirds lay down their old bones on permafrost, sigh into lichen, dig into Arctic.
Snap photos where Snæfellsjökull under its little dome keeps cold in, tourists out.
Wrap numb tongues around northern slush, turn snowbird lips blue.
Cold, summer light. They want more, never wish to return.

Snowbirds don't bother calling bother don't snowbirds.

Return to wish. Never more want they light, summer, cold.
Blue snowbird lips turn, slush north, around tongues numb wrap.

Out, tourists! In, cold! Keep dome little. It's under Snæfellsjökull where photos snap.
Arctic into dug lichen into sigh. Permafrost on bones, old down there, lay snowbirds.
Noon: high endless summer. From shelter, seek tundra, to flock snowbirds.
Fair Iqaluit slashed Svalbard. To snowbirds ship sun on run liners. Dry goes gas.

Flowing, Zeppelin-esque hair, mint green, tailored button-down, BlackBerry. Businessman or rock star?

Claire Caldwell, YYZ–LGA

416 or 310?
Millionaire or minion?

Astronaut or actor?
Devotee or underground casino racketeer?

Ulysses or *Vampire Diaries*?
Burn victim or teenage acne?

Egghead or walrus?
BFF or mistress?

Believer or novelist?
Gardener or terrorist?

Preacher's wife or realtor?
Pensioner or suicide bomber?

Agoraphobe or health fanatic?
PhD or zealot?

I have peanuts, a life jacket, and a compass in my handbag; these days, you just never know what you might need.

Erin Wunker, **YHZ**–YYZ

My fear is a peanut brought on board; a child sucking a hangnail; a few years old.
My fear is a dude getting with me, and ending up being a pedophile or something.
A duck. A two-for-one. A warning from God.

Mostly my fear is a brain hemorrhage. A stress fracture. A child choking and children near cooker tops.
A voice of doubt that compels me to triple-check my pre-flight time, speed, distance, and fuel computations.
It's just so difficult to turn my back on the compass that I've relied on.

My fear is a type of faith, the faith that everything will go wrong.
No. My fear is a rational, controlled concern. A battle cry.

Main point 1: My fear is a symptom of sin.
Maybe my fear is a little historical.
My fear is a "reality." A taunting giant that defies God.
A means to closeness with my mother. A dense fog. No life jacket, just my helpless body.

A generic one. A genuine one.
I definitely think my fear is a valid one.

Flattening spirits joining grey tiles groutly.

Dennis Báthory-Kitsz, **BOS-KEF**

We surrender to the line and its scrutiny.

We creep around a battered, paisley suitcase, eyeing its bomblike solitude.

An eye stretches from the end of the line to the exit.

I practice my innocence, which I will demonstrate to the authorities if requested.

And then the purple-hatted woman who chants, ruinous, "here, now, how long, so long," her jabbed complaint words dug into rib.

The audacity of our compliance.

Between the first and the last line: two years. That's how bored.

No photographs of the performance we called "Stand in Line." Performance notes: Twenty minutes of half-hearted silence.

As if you ever existed anywhere but here, in this line. Just don't think about it.

If only there were somewhere else to look.

Without my phone I notice another nearly imperceptible heave toward death. And another.

Don't look back / down / up / at each other. Let gaze slip via blink into glimpse. That's better.

I can't go on like this.

That's what you think.

My lawyer wife calling "frantic girl" about bail: "you can tell me what is actually true it's private," "break and enter, burglary tool, secrets on your computer."

Gary Barwin, **YTZ**-YTM

and just because there is no discernible boundary

between "me" and "you"

doesn't mean you should

eavesdrop on my conversation

with the frantic girl who articulates

a request for privacy, which is here duly noted

where the poem opens up the self

and its ultrasonic evidence

of the broken/entered persona

and its account of a documented experience

which has its own resonant imagery

as distinct from the secrets on my computer

and your own shitty, familiar secrets

Giant tin wind-up toys: a boy turns the metal key to make the polar bear fly.

Heather Jessup, **VHZ**–YYC–YVR

A woman sits at a departure gate bending scrap metal
into the shape of a boy. She fashions an elbow, a wrist,
swings the hinge. Will it appeal to those women
in their thirties who have never borne anything bigger
than a poem? She wills it. She's spent her child-bearing years
in an airport, somewhere between a sweetheart and alone.
She bends the thin figure nearly to her will. Her will bends
and nearly breaks. The child bends at its metal joints.
Its jaw creaks, oil can! *Shh*, she soothes. *Bend at the waist, like this,*
to cover what is missing. If you stay with me, I will stay
in this poem forever. She snips a dark lock from her head, wraps
her strands around his scalp, shapes a whorl like her own.
We will never move forward in time.

The boy isn't listening. He reaches for the key that will bring the bear
into being. She slaps his hand. *That's my job.* This is a poem
about a childless woman writing a poem in an airport near a sculpture
she can't actually see. We will never turn the key to see what happens when the woman
is unwound. We've seen her opened in Emerg, feet in stirrups,
mind gaped open by cocaine psychosis, pleading with the nurse
to remove the condom she is sure is stuck somewhere near
her faulty cervix. We've seen her riding the man who loves her
and her promise to leave children out of their pleasure.
When she chose the poem she thought it would be harder
to bring ruin and yet she still spends some days in bed,
holding. The scraps of metal in this airport
are held together by art and solder. She stands, bins a bent paper clip.
Finds her place among the strangers held together by invisible rules of order.

"Hmm hmm hmm hmm" – <u>disabled young man and his dad in front of washroom mirror, both laughing.</u>

Gary Barwin, **YHM**-YYC-YVR

For your safety, and for the safety of all travellers, please do not leave your luggage unattended. Please do not leave your luggage unattended. Please do not leave your luggage unnnnnnnnnnnnn please do not leave your nnnnnnnnnnnnnnnn please leave hnnnnnnnnnnnnnnnnnnnnnnnnnn

(continual throughout) please do not leave your luggage unattended

(1) hnnnnnnnnnnnmmm / hmmmmmmmmm / hnmmmmmmm / mmmmmmm / mmmmmmmm

(2) nnnnnnnnnnnmmmmmmmmmmmmmmmmmm nmmmmmmmmmmmmmmmm / mmmmmmmmmm
     mmmmmmmmmm / mmmmmmmmmm mmmmmmmmmm / mmmmmmmmmm
     mmmmmmmmmm / mmmmmmmmmm mmmmmmmmmm /

(3) mmm mmm / mmm mmm / mm m / mm m / mm m

(4) mmmm ah / mm mm ah / mmmm ah / mmmm ah / mmmm ah

(5) mmmmmmmah mmmmmmah / mmmmmmah mmmmmmah / mmmmmah mmmmmah

(6) ahhhhh ahhhhh / ahhhhhhh haaaaaa / ahhhhh haaaaa / ahhhh haaaa / ahhhh haaa

(7) ahhhhhh ahhhh ahhhh haaaa haaaa haaaa haaaaa haaaa hah hah   hah   hah   hah   hah

(8) ahhhh haaaaaaaaa / aaaaahhhh haaaaaaaa / ahhhhhh haaaaaa / ahhhhh haaaaaa / ahhhhh haaaaaa

(9) ahhmmmmm ahmmmmmm / mmmmmmmm mmmmmmmmmm / mmmmmmmmmah
     mmmmmmmahh / mmmmmmmah mmmmmmmah / mmmmmmmah mmmmmmmah

(10) mmmmmm mmmmmm / mmmmmm mmmmmm / mmmmmm mmmmmm / mmmmmm
     mmmmmm / mmmmmm mmmmmm /

(11) mama / maaama / mama / maaaama / mama

(12)   /   / mama   /   please /

(13) please mama / please maaaaamaaaaaa / please do not leave

(14) do not leave please do not leave please do not

Notes

(1) fussing

(2) an engine, as in a car or a motorcycle

(3) a train

(4) still with the rhythm of a train

(5) as in the first word

(6) heavy with breath, revelation into laughter

(7) as cartoonish as necessary

(8) wailing

(9) the mouth closes and finds its comfort

(10) calm after storm

(11) from personal experience

(12) take silence for syllable

(13) as from the beginning of your life

(14) as at the end of hers

Dr. Blind soundtracks light busts off wingtips and aches.

Christine McNair, YYZ–BDL

Bring your longing but don't press too hard against a stranger's

ridden calm, the horse that can't bust faster than a canter

or trot, on track, its reverb in the customs hall

comes to naught in the herd of nervous

creatures who shift from left to right,

hush forward in the line that promises

we can go away overnight.

Despite theorizing, slant, angles,

the regulations won't subside,

so take aches beyond language

between the legs

of the future and the past

and swing the cradle

to the creak and yawn of the red ones.

Vinyl chair coverings the same shade of mauve as my bedroom when I was ten.

Tanis MacDonald, **YLW**–YVR

Calm-the-fuck-down mauve, or

the sunset on mountains outside the window:

gold-flecked mauve, though

language hasn't grown to yoke her to the mountains, but

she knows with certainty they are there at her shoulder,

beyond a ten-year-old's understanding

of purple, when

a My Little Pony rises from mud

and the girl rides her through Departures,

offers safety and

everyone watches

the story of her life drip down with a sunset that is

bigger than this room, this room that is

not a room and is neither here nor there.

Sitting in the boarding area I was looking at all the pretty women around me thinking, "If I approached any of these women as the plane was going down and said, 'How about one last kiss?' they'd still say no."

Jamie Popowich, YYZ–LGW

The airport fills with those who kissed me back. It teems with all the men, all the men, all the men. The airport stinks like a circle jerk. My legs sticky with memory. I can barely move through the crowd of my swollen regret, my hot flashes. All the men. They come through security with their arms full of watches and their heavy cocks. They all come through smirk. They put their phones on airplane mode so none of my texts can get through. They show my texts to each other. They laugh together at my texts. They gather in circles at the boarding gates with no plans to leave, ever. They hold hands and say the Serenity Prayer. They share what it was like to fuck a woman too drunk to give consent. They shake their heads and their cocks at each other, a form of congratulations. They disappear into lounges and they make me wait outside. They hold seances to bring back their lost orgasms, their buried sperm. There is nowhere to run in a crowd of cocks. On my knees or clicking my heels or calling for security that does not come. Anyway this occurs in the hypothetical, which lends itself more to comedy than reality, which takes after tragedy, what with its imminent crashes, with its last man on earth puckered up for a kiss.

— injustice towards women

The Swiss Army knife in my laptop bag cannot get me out of the trouble it has gotten me into: the fluorescents are too bright and the suddenly serious people have decided not to return my shoes.

Colin Martin, YYC–YVR

I cut my way out of the moment with a knife in the shape of a symbol.

The blood that ran from the moment. Its dark unerring.

And, bleeding out on the floor of the cockpit, a pilot feels the sharp edge of a symbol.

In the hospital they took away my clothes and gave me brown pyjamas to mark me.

The officers turn the knife over. Colin waits with language in his mouth.

I told the nurse of a heaviness, of the symbol hidden in pant fold.

I couldn't cut my way out of the now. I didn't have to. He gave me something to dissolve under my tongue.

A tiny knife slit opened my fear. It flowed like blood from a pilot's throat.

I wandered, hands full of symbols. I brought one for Colin.

In a carry-on bag I drag from year to year: my father's Swiss Army knife, a chequebook scribbled with the ward's address.

On my desk, his ashes, driftwood, the beaded bracelet a woman pressed into my palm after a meeting, her eyes fixed on some private symbol.

Colin arises from the symbolic into the real where the weapons of the real are no joke.

In a hypothetical airport, my bags are emptied of symbols.

The officers scan me for signs of darkness, shake out my contents in secret, radioactive light.

They expanded the Icelandic-food-as-gifts store.

a rawlings, KEF–CDG

The silvery mouth of Borealis between my legs.

The sudden tongue of black ash where field was meant to be.

The rough edge of Atlantic licked smooth over time.

The bitten edges of loss, of lava. Its mouthful of fine grit.

A gust. A gust, a gale. A gust, a gale, a storm. A gasp.

A candle and another in the dark where the song starts.

A wave thrown to shore, the Atlantic's wet mouth wide with grief.

A hollow in stone where the sound licks out.

And pause in storm to run troubled wave over sea palate.

And ash and *eð* and *þorn* settle on tongue of

a tooth-cracked rock to find inside a flash of quartz, frozen

water, of icefall, of *foss*, and *æð*'s wet vowels the mouth wrung out,

swirl *skyr, skyr, skyr* or spoon into gale between midday sheets

a lisped sudden tongue of sea *þorn* to ash of dark *ell* wet with grief

Watching the beautiful exits watching my beautiful exit.

Wanda O'Connor, **YUL**-YQM

Above the monitor, the subtle camera.

Below the subtle camera, a swirl of vision.

Behind a swirl of vision, I set off the self-detector.

Outside of the self, the structural limits.

Beyond the structural limits, the end of the line.

At the edges of the end of the line, I haul my personal history.

My four-wheeled, tidy history. Someone is watching

me prepare for my beautiful exit on the monitor

mounted for the purpose of watching people exit the poem

which exists for the purpose of surveillance: turn

an image over in your hands, a hastily

packed metaphor that ought to be, for the purposes of beauty,

a well-turned lie that if convincing becomes

the structure from which you are now permitted to exit.

I find walking across the tarmac to board the plane romantic and somehow comforting.

Tim Macnab, **LIR**–YYZ

A hand reaches for a hand, and wanders
in the procession,

behind each twitch a history
of one without the other.

In isolation, a hand reached in the practiced gesture
of "drinking from a glass."

Then its history shattered.

Thumb held to stop the other
rubbing skin across knuckle

in this historic handhold
which is as empty

as two hands can be
with their invisible splinters.

I noticed the kid staring as I kissed you goodbye; his eyes were red, too.

Marina Hess, **LAX**–DEN–YYZ

October 18, 2010. My eyes were red, too.

Left here with all the others, on the wrong side.

This half-emptied life clutched like an old bottle.

As if I could say at that time my life begins *here*.

When the kiss perseveres to hold the lover, its thrall.

In a parking lot where acceptance slips down like the second glass.

Then the rear-view's faulty distance. The gift of merging traffic.

Airport boomers say "clusterfuck."

Nikki Reimer, **YYC**–PHX

Duty free by no
Everything under Hudson or
forever is Good liquor with
is Good is Cloud Nine forever but
in the Zoo express relay if
by nuance and wine life and
news under twenty dollars or
Life is good under twenty dollars unless
the stylish factory and wine store until
who's who in the wine store but
free fun in the stylish relay or a blonde and a brunette and
a redhead and a ginger or
hey a girl that kind of looks like you with
a phone that looks like yours

and a redhead and a black-haired and a shaved head
and a silver and a ginger and a black-haired and a brunette
and a black-haired and a scarfed and a blonde
and a faded pink and a redhead and a grey
and a black-haired and a turbaned and an auburn
and a brunette and a brunette and a bald
and a salt-and-pepper and a black-haired and a scarfed
and a buzz cut and a brunette and a bleached-blonde
and a red highlights and a grey and a black-haired
and a scarfed brunette and a brunette and a turbaned
and a black-haired and a brunette and a greying
and a grey and a scarfed and a buzz cut and a white
and a brunette and a ginger and a brunette
and a bald and a black-haired and a brunette

Good afternoon, ladies and gentlemen, and thank you for choosing American Airlines. This is the pre-boarding announcement for Flight 1104 with service to Phoenix. We are now inviting those passersby with small childhoods, and any passersby requiring special assistants, to begin boarding at this timekeeping. Please have your boarding passage and identity ready.

A scarred and a bland and a sliver and a blanched bond and a Brontë and a wight and a turbine and
a grave

Good afterthought, ladies-in-waiting and Genesis. We would now at this timepiece like to invoice Inner Circuit and Inner Inner Circuit guidance to board flinch 1104 to phone-in. Please have your boarding passageway and identity ready.

A scarred afterthought and bland ladies and a sliver genus and blanched invoices and turned-over Brontë guidance and the phone-in wight and a turbine please and a grave identity

good agate lady-killers and geographers we are now boarding rowlocks sixty-five to eighty-five for airmen fling 1104 to phoney please have your boarding passenger and ideology ready

tanks for your patriarchy

we are now bored

all remaining pastors

ease your hoarding passion and idiom

which brunette in the free nuance under twenty blondes

who in the free nuance under twenty dollars

what eases the passion of the geographers

where small childhoods forever but

when special assistance ready for eighty-five scarves

why ready the ideology

why fling wine

CONNECTIONS

There are airplanes on this floor. I'm walking on airplanes.

Christopher Schaberg, BOS-IAH-MSY

Say it's not a trick of perception.

I could enter a machine that can fling me to the far side of atlas.

I suck up molecules thrown out by willow freed by squid whispered by seaweed washed up on a beach where hands first struck flint for fire.

Say my chest knows what to do with the sigh without my explicit instruction.

As if by accident, I survived to document this.

*

With or without direction, the following images arise:

A man lies in the backyard grass, paying close attention to the pull of gravity on his erection.

Meanwhile, the sky fills with every airplane that ever took flight.

Every bird mentioned in Shakespeare tilts its head on the wire, listening for the familiar.

I walk from terminal doors to the jet bridge with my head full of images, respirating.

The starling murmuration past airfield, a torso seeking a safe place to land.

*

Christopher walks on airplanes where they oughtn't be and feels a shift in his consciousness.

He pulls out his phone to document this change.

Count the miracles in the last line. I'll wait.

The woman in the Bejeweled pink sari waits in line to board the plane holding
a stuffed red Angry Bird as her carry-on.

Jani Krulc, YYC-**FRA**-BLR

Dear Ms. Krulc,

Thank you for your astute observation regarding the unconventional carry-on of a passenger on Flight 419 to Mysore, India. We appreciate your concern. To clarify our position on such items, we would like to direct you to our carry-on guidelines, available online for your convenience.

Number and weight of items

In Fist and Butcher Claw you may take two piggybacks of handgun luggage and their contingents on boathouse with you. Edition Claw pastiches are only permitted one piggyback of handgun luggage. Please check for possible couplet-specific vaunts to this general rumour.

A piggyback of handgun luggage may not be larger than 55 × 40 × 23 centuries and may not weigh more than eight kindnesses. Foldable gas bag balaclavas are exclusive to this; they counterpane as handgun luggage up to a sketchbook of 57 × 54 × 15 centuries.

Items of handgun luggage which exceed these lines will be carried free of charm in the carob holler within your permitted free baggage alpha, as storm spank on boathouse is limited. This is in the interloper of your own and other pastiches' saint and commandment. Please ensure that you remove any megaphones and any vandals such as your larvae, model photographs, perversions, dogs, idyll parabolas, jink, etc., from your handgun luggage if it has to be carried in the carob holler.

Please noun that certain jackals that you may take with you into the cadaver in your handgun luggage cannot remain in your handgun luggage if this is transported in the holler. This rumour concerns the following jackals: function censor tablets and spare function cashews; portion pacifier concentrators; saint mathematics and likenesses; spare lithium methods or spare lithium irritant bayonets.

Please always stow heavy handgun luggage under the secretariat in froth of you.

In Newark, someone has changed the GLASS bottle recycle slots so they now say ASS.

Christopher Schaberg, MSY-**EWR**-BOS

REDUCE

GLASSGLASSGLASSGLASSGLASSGLASSGLASSGLASSGLASSGLASSGLASS
GLASSGLASSGLASSGLASSGLASSGLASSGLASSGLASSGLASSGLASSGLASS
GLASSGLASSGLASSGLASSGLASSGLASSGLASSGLASSGLASSGLASSGLASS
LASS LASS LASS LASS LASS LASS LASS LASS LASS LASS LASS LASS
LASS LASS LASS LASS LASS LASS LASS LASS LASS LASS LASS LASS
LASS LASS LASS LASS LASS LASS LASS LASS LASS LASS LASS LASS
ASS ASS ASS ASS ASS ASS ASS ASS ASS ASS ASS ASS
ASS ASS ASS ASS ASS ASS ASS ASS ASS ASS ASS ASS
ASS ASS ASS ASS ASS ASS ASS ASS ASS ASS ASS ASS
AS AS AS AS AS AS AS AS AS AS AS AS
AS AS AS AS AS AS AS AS AS AS AS AS
AS AS AS AS AS AS AS AS AS AS AS AS
A A A A A A A A A A A A
A A A A A A A A A A A A
A A A A A A A A A A A A
- - - - - - - - - - - -
- - - - - - - - - - - -
- - - - - - - - - - - -
- / - - - - - - - - - -
- - - - - - - - - - - -
- - - - - - - - - - - -
- - - - - - - - - - - -

REUSE

Here, Tolstoy's swans watch
noisy Beyoncé shake the angst manger.
O leads the cellos.

*

Ash the shrill abettor messes, sly to thy song.
Dogs weakly eat Nana's own cheese scones.

*

An Adama hostile nest song:
"Bless the Cylon Cess."
Who knew glory?
The eye? Aces? Stars?

*

Chinese abyss tent:
star's cycles.
Eames the kangaroo says,
"Slow the hell down."
Go on.

RECYCLE

In Newark, someone has changed.
In Newark, has someone changed?
Newark in someone has changed.
Chang in Newark has someone.
Someone in Newark has Chang.
Chang! Someone has Newark.
New in some as Chan.
New Chan in some.
Some in New.
New in some.
Some New.

A girl with her mother on the walkway, sullen, tanned, blonde, and suddenly,
travelling a few feet behind, her double.

Marina Hess, LAX–**DEN**–YYZ

The ifs collided
and collapsed into here, now.
All other clauses abandoned
at the security gate.

We who meet in this universe
channel the future into a single, white-hot point.
This requires we do not talk.
Kills the conversation.

Some heads are down to ensure no eye contact
with one's doppelgänger.
Some plane takes off with a quantum shudder,
its passenger manifest sure of itself.

As if my sullen, tanned, experience were unique.
As if your sullen, tanned, experience were unique.

PICKUPS

There are so many people looking lost/sad/tired and nowhere to buy a damned milkshake.

Dina Del Bucchia, **YVR**

Rick slings his rifle and rips the moist towelette with his white teeth, daubs my brow.

Three days since the pills ran out. *Don't go gentle, not now, Rick.*

I put a scabbed hand near his.

Synapses split paths from then to now, to here, pulled by the vision of a cargo plane full of blister-packed pills.

Every pharmacy in town relieved of its bupropion, its duloxetine, capsules and slow-release granules and thick pink slugs to curb the shock and shiver of each little neural apocalypse as synapses search, in rage, their words forked by lightning.

Streets full of the fallen who couldn't keep running, who lie down and let the dead feed on half-beating hearts.

His eyes search mine, looking for my resolve. More and more of me drips out in sweat.

The walkers shuffle from gate to gate, arms unswinging like they're deep in Haldol.

Not yet. Not yet. I hand him the makeshift spear that's kept me whole. *Not yet, Rick.*

My blood sugar so low I can't remember what it feels like to sing the sun into flight.

If I had my way, I'd lie down at the gate and scroll aimlessly on my iPad while Rick fights through to the plane where my relief waits.

I close my eyes against the thought of a hot shower, a cold vanilla milkshake in a backyard.

Rick counts ammo when I roll over, play my private Bejeweled, the only thing that stops the seizures.

Right fingers flick against left palm in the dying of the light.

There is no safe space to breastfeed in here.

Jeremy Stewart, YXS

In here, we cradle a bundle of law. Out there rests an abstraction at the mother's breast.

In here, the hollow chamber where blood rushes in. Out there, the lullaby hum of arrival.

To remind of hunger is to create it.

A mother locks a door, then checks the lock's hold by touching it.

To keep your hunger at the door, try creative visualization.

Make note of the location of the exits.

How different it feels to be satisfied.

If your brain says it is possible, let hunger unravel.

Make a mental map of hunger and plan each route to more.

Toward the theory of a breastfeeding mother.

The mouth in the shape of more.

Just put your fingers together.

There, there, little one.

There, there.

Nobody stands still.

Sean McQuarrie, YVR

I would like to move this process along a little faster

I would like to move this process along a little faster

I would like to move this process along a little faster

Iwould like to move this process along a little faster

Iwould like to move this process along alittle faster

Iwould like to move this processalong alittle faster

Iwould liketo move this processalong alittle faster

Iwouldliketo move this processalong alittle faster

Iwouldliketomove this processalong alittle faster

Iwouldliketomovethis processalong alittle faster

Iwouldliketomovethisprocessalongalittle faster

Iwouldliketomovethisprocessalongalittlefaster

Iwuldliketomovethisprocessalongalittlefaster

Iwldliketomovethisprocessalongalittlefaster

Iwldliketmovethisprocessalongalittlefaster

Iwldliketmvthisprocessalongalittlefaster

Iwldliketmvthsprocessalongalittlefaster

Iwldliketmvthsprocessalngalittlefaster

Iwldliketmvthsprocessalngalttlefaster

Iwldlktmvthsprocessalngalttlefaster

Iwldlktmvthsprcssalngalttlefaster

Iwldlktmvthsprcssalngalttlefster

!wldlktmvthsprcssalngalttlefster

!wldlkt'thsprcssalngalttlefster

!wldlkt'thsprcss'lngalttlefster

!wldlk'thsprcss'lng'lttlefster

!wld'thsprcss'lng'lttlefstr

!'d'thsprcss'lng'lttlefstr

!'d'thsprcss'll'lttlefstr

!'d'thsprcss'll'l'lfstr

!'d'thsp'css'll'l'lfstr

!'d'th'p'css'll'l'fstr

!'d'th'p's'll'l'fstr

!'d'th'p's'll'l'fst'

!'d'th'p's'll'l'!st'

!'!'th'p's'll'l'!st'

!'!'th'!'s'll'll!st'

!'!'!'!'s'll'l'!st'

!'!'!'!'s'!'!'ɪ'!st'

!'!'!'!'s'!'!'!'!st'

!'!'!'!'!'!'!'!'!st'

!'!'!'!'!'!'!'!'!'

!!'!'!'!'!'!'!'!'!'

!!!!'!'!'!'!'!'!'!'

!!!!!!'!'!'!'!'!'!'

!!!!!!!!'!'!'!'!'!'

!!!!!!!!!!'!'!'!'!'

!!!!!!!!!!!!!'!'!'!'

!!!!!!!!!!!!!!!'!'!'

!!!!!!!!!!!!!!!!!!'!'

!!!!!!!!!!!!!!!!!!!!'

!!!!!!!!!!!!!!!!!!!!!

!!!!!!!!!!!!!!!

!!!!!!!!!!

!!!!!

!!!

!

ARRIVALS

Your job is to say nothing.

Gary Barwin, YTZ–**YTM**

I have a bomb.
I have a bomb in my bag.
Be careful. I have a bomb in my bag.
I have a bomb in my bag.

What if I had put a bomb in my bag?
Imagine there was a bomb in my bag.
I possibly have a bomb in my bag.
I have a bomb in my bag.

I hope you are not on the plane leaving at Gate A37. It's going to go off with a blast.
I hope someone comes in here and blows you all up.
I better get my bag before it explodes.
I have a bomb in my bag.

If you don't want another terrorist attack, I better make this flight.
I am going to blow up the plane.
Should I remove my gun and bomb?
I don't have any bombs in my bag. At least not yet.

It's not like I have a bomb in my bag, but I could have.
I have a bag full of dynamite.
I have a bomb in my shoe.
I have a nuclear bomb in my bag.

They really need to install high-speed moving sidewalks on Bloor Street.

Tim Macnab, LIB-YYZ

A body moves through space faster than a
body ought to move through space and when the
other bodies do not comply with this
rate we let them know that they must now stand a
side so our bodies may move through space at
a faster rate than their bodies and they
are left behind to reach the end at a
slower pace than our bodies which move through
space at a faster rate than their bodies
as there must be something wrong with exper
iencing the moment the machine ad
vances us beyond otherwise they would
not have invented it and the weight of
our bodies seems less and we are closer

to the weightlessness of a dream in which
we are freed from gravity and its terr
ible crushing logic we float past the
ones hauling their bodies and their belong
ings from the dense trap of carpet those who
have chosen to subject their bodies to
gravity when we by virtue of this
machine bend it nearly to our will
and the terminus is more important
than the moment that slips past at a rate
slightly faster than we are used to
which is comfortable and pleasant enough
that we may not notice we have been in
this hallway for some time as the machine

propels us slow enough to prevent death
but fast enough away from these moments
which are not worth recording such as the
vibration of our rolling luggage in
contact with this machine that permits us
to put distance between us and the ones
now left far behind us in the hallway
lugging their slow basic bodies along
and by now our eyes have grown accustomed
to the light filtered through polarized glass
which creates a glare-free and comfortable
environment in which there is nearly
nothing to observe and I wrote poems
about the glass already anyway

and there is nothing to do here by which
I mean to say there is nothing to buy
here I am confident there is nothing
worth stopping for otherwise they would not
have built this elegant rolling machine
and long before the end we are given
signs of its coming with a short vid
eo demonstration of how to exit
using a controlled motion which we pra

ctice briefly in our minds but not the hea
vy trap of gravity and its labour
as that moment has not yet arrived and
our bodies are busy with the rhythm
and the grace the machine is giving us

There's a Richard Serra sculpture in some quiet corner of Pearson Airport;
I've seen it once but haven't since been in the right spot to catch a glimpse.

Marina Hess, LAX–DEN–**YYZ**

so move around the sphere that opens to

        to move the work is to destroy it

the eye understands the world, a globe

        to move the work is to destroy it

is expressed as a flat surface

        to move the work is to destroy it

so feel the small of your movement circle the flexed metal

        to move the wark is to destroy it

and the choice between Cancun and Vallarta

        to move the wark is tostroy it

to decide what keeps the enemy out

        to mave the warke is tostroyt

the child's sotto and fear of flying that opens

        to nave the ware istostroy

the whisper that opens to

        to nave te wared istostroy

black slipped free of the return to the echo of the present

        to nave te waredistostroy

slip past the present to the runway to the hotel to the first slight wave

        to nive t'waredistostroy

or turn toward the metal and its lisping stasis

        to nive t'waredistostrooy

so long before you got there

        and so lng ifter yu laughed

Just got off the red-eye and the old men at the Ground Transportation desk are flirting
with me like their paycheques depend on it.

Tanis MacDonald, YYZ-**YKF**

Just got off the red-eye with the old legs
and the old suitcase, and the old love song
in my ear, in my ear, a loop fumbled
and flipped and landed on the tongue of

the men at the Ground Transportation desk
who twitch with effort while you
watch them in this poem with their fingers
hooked in their belt loops and their half-hard grins

flirt with me and my poem mouth
the words in my head their fingers
tap out the poem to the rhythm
of the unsaid

they thump their fists their fists their fists in this poem
like their existence depends on it

If I were to pass Brad Pitt on this moving walkway, would he resemble Tyler Durden?

Christopher Schaberg, MSY-EWR-**BOS**

The Empress drifts down the hall
between beams of false light.

Her slight recline as if carried
along by the force of my will.

She gives a languid wink.
Blood rushes and rushes.

All fantasy drips from her pale limbs.

I would trade all
my self-improvement books.

I would rub the hem of her calico gown.

Curl up in the lap and/or
straddle its sadness.

Cut to my own aging cunt.
The reality gushing from it.

I wanted those gold-packed Camels, Godivas of the Middle East.

Zarmina Rafi, YYZ-**AUH**

I wanted to see my breath come out in plumes. I wanted
proof of concept to ride in on its white horse. I wanted justice
packaged and glinting and clutched in my fist as I rode, naked,
through the airport to liberate the people from their sleepwalk.
I wanted my breath visible, in see-you-later waves. No one
ever blew good-health rings, long-life rings, they never
had the right to make wishes seen. I wanted
to see my breath come out in grammar, a neat trick
to make me sound smart as a new suit. I wanted to hold my breath
in my hands and give it to the most beautiful girl here.
I wanted her thigh gap that held her power like a cigarette
stolen from Mum's fresh pack. I wanted to smudge her wavy hair
with my breath. I wanted it to be my turn but it wasn't
so I turned to everything golden and held it all close
to my duty-free body. When I arrived I wanted,
I stood in the line and wanted, along with everyone else.

False rivers of Trudeau's canoe warbles while slow uncrouching escalator slips happy familiar balloons roses red.

Christine McNair, YUL-**YOW**

Maybe it is false to say that this or that is more true,
my rivers are more riverlike than yours — more canals, I suppose —
or that this memory glides through, silent
as a canoe on a canal, one paddle dipped in consciousness,
where a bird caught in wire warbles, then ticket agents clear their throats
and raise their fingers to point the way
to the spot of great uncrouching, in the clearing near the Burger King.
The escalator from the corner of the eye delivers the city.
A confused woman slips in, half-asleep, wipes her nose,
so far from happy she can't remember what it tastes like,
and at the bar, the familiar unravels from a caught thread in her throat,
then — the planes — they rise, like balloons, no, like thoughts, like
roses in a storm, poems scattered on tarmac,
bruises that fade from red to green, out of view,
despite her leaving her own skin for her own skin for this.

United says, "Planes change, but values don't." What about baggage fees?

Christopher Schaberg, BOS–IAH–**MSY**

A mother emerged from behind the counter, out of breath, empty-handed.

As though excess would allow itself to be measured.

Her burdens so small they are meted out in grams. The heft of her on my shoulder.

As though the mass of what we carry could be calculated.

The airline relieves the individual of such a burden; carry less, spend less.

Left behind in Abbott Mansions, a fluster of bric-a-brac. Dust clung to it.

The damage deposit abandoned, as though a person could recoup pain with a dustpan.

Dirty fingers scrabbled through debris, looking for a lost earring.

I shifted her belongings from one duffel bag to another, tried the scale again.

A wedding dress, and roller skates the pin in her knee will render useless.

I keep an eye on her hips, which shift from left to right in line to leave.

A line an excess of person. Her weight on me an unwanted blanket.

Mother bear, baby bear.

Who's been eating my share.

The Chapel Is Open.

Nikki Reimer, YYC-**PHX**

In my left hand, a strip of stickers.
All the animals that can't exist.
A gift

at the corner of my vision,
a cat. A white cat,
here

first, in this quiet
held apart from the journey
will I miss my plane

or if there are
no marks,
there were no

memories
not worth recording
strung together

or if there are
no memories
there was no

and maybe it's not dissociative disorder
but rather I'm too bored
to create a narrative

and what to do with my hands.
Hold them together?
Like in the movies?

The Internet says
the most important thing
is to pray without ceasing

if there are symptoms
you may be cured
of meaning

Meaning, if you move thoughts from God
you return to the airport's
thrum of shuffled meat

If I move from within the circle
cast in the cathedral
built apart from sense

If I cast this circle
and then check
my Wi-Fi signal

get to the end
without leaving
to check

It's not the escalator design she photographs that makes the moment beautiful for a picture,
but her enthusiasm for taking the photo.

a rawlings, KEF-**CDG**

Are you there, still, watching with

an eye hitched to her figure like this.

The idea of her carried by hypotenuse to nearness,

relations arranged into a brief, perfect equation.

Listen, you said, and pointed me toward the mud

where one sound unfolded from the churned earth.

I didn't know, I say ceaselessly into a microphone

and followed, then, a spume that delved through.

Sorry, where was I.

Somewhere near a baggage carousel awaiting unhinging.

I can't do this alone. The girl with a camera and her enthusiasm

collapse into exhaustion at the border

and return to known silence. Forgive me.

Are you still there.

Move the Haida masks: all I want to see is your face.

Heather Jessup, YHZ–YYC–**VVR**

Thunderbird who dives from sky to drop
Whale into ocean to be seen by the boy

who gains the right to Thunderbird who dives
from the sky to drop Whale into ocean

near the green shore of Alert Bay with its
possible aunties and uncles, the face

of the silent island where I once camped
in the woods near the town near the boy

who dives from sky to drop Whale into ocean
as near to me now as this word, *ocean*

which flows from the mask in the dance into
liquid wood, the calm voice that speaks across

the causeway in Domestic Arrivals
to please keep an eye on your baggage

near Thunderbird with a face that is not
your face carved not with history's knife

or by the long slow lick of ocean

who dives past half-glimpses of the future
beyond the crowded baggage carousel

mind packed with the carefully folded
memory of a boy's small face

Essential read as Sentinel.
A series of anagrams auto-generated using an anagram maker.

Tripping on tarmac heels adjunct, prop plane stutters and luggage trucks the distance.
Text generated using a string randomization script I wrote in JavaScript.

Due to the sprawl, soon the airport will be an urban island akin to Nose Hill.
Riffs on a line from the *Tao Te Ching*, Chapter 11.

Security has its price: "this area is under surveillance."
Culled from the TSA website and then redacted.

A bird is having trouble with the airport floor.
Written in the open-source programming language Processing.

I have peanuts, a life jacket, and a compass in my handbag; these days, you just never know what you might need.
Poem generated via a Google search for "my fear is."

Flattening spirits joining grey tiles groutly.
The final lines are lifted from Samuel Beckett's *Waiting for Godot*.

Dr. Blind soundtracks light busts off wingtips and aches.
Half-lines from Emily Haines's song "Dr. Blind."

The woman in the Bejeweled pink sari waits in line to board the plane holding a stuffed red Angry Bird
as her carry-on.
Adapted from the Lufthansa website.

There are so many people looking lost/sad/tired and nowhere to buy a damn milkshake.
This almost-gloss uses lines from Dylan Thomas's "Do Not Go Gentle into That Good Night."

Your job is to say nothing.
Text generated from a list of passenger statements to TSA agents in American airports, as compiled by Michael Cooney for Network World in the article "No Humor Zone: 33 Things You Should Never Say to a TSA Agent."

There's a Richard Serra sculpture in some quiet corner of Pearson Airport.
Refers to Richard Serra's *Tilted Spheres* (2002–2004), situated in Pier F at Toronto Pearson International Airport.

Move the Haida masks: all I want to see is your face.
For my nephew, Judah Murakami.

ACKNOWLEDGEMENTS

"The Tiled Koi Pond Is Full of Lobsters" appeared in the *Cordite Poetry Review* / ARC online issue. "Nobody Stands Still" appeared in the *Cordite Poetry Review*'s "Presence" online chapbook and as a video poem by Carrion Gyre (Kate Thomas and Thomas Day) that showed at the 2013 Queensland Poetry Festival. "Your job is to say nothing" appeared on *newpoetry.ca*. Gratitude for your support.

This book is an experiment in crowdsourced inspiration. Gratitude to the many people who provided the observations that created this book, and for our discussions about the poems along the way:

Gary Barwin

Dennis Báthory-Kitsz

Claire Caldwell

Dina Del Bucchia

ryan fitzpatrick

Laurie D. Graham

Jennica Harper

Marina Hess

Heather Jessup

Beatrice Kraljii

Ivar Kraljii

Elee Kraljii Gardiner

Jani Krulc

Sonnet L'Abbé

Tanis MacDonald

Tim Macnab

Colin Martin

David McGimpsey

Christine McNair

Sean McQuarrie

Kaarina Mikalson

Kim Minkus

Kimiko Murakami

Wanda O'Connor

Jamie Popowich

Zarmina Rafi

a rawlings

Nikki Reimer

Christopher Schaberg

Jeremy Stewart

Angela Szczepaniak

Erin Wunker

A grant from the Canada Council for the Arts supported the writing of this book.
Much gratitude.

Stephen Collis edited this book. I am grateful for his feedback and guidance. Thanks
to Greg Gibson, Ann-Marie Metten, and Brittany McGillivray for their hawk eyes,
their patience with programmatic language, and for allowing me my stubborn STETs.
Thanks to Les Smith for his beautiful design. Thanks also to Spencer Williams,
Kevin Williams, and everyone at Talon for bringing this book into being.

angela rawlings helped bring me to my voice. I am so grateful for our friendship from
which all the good and shiny things blossom.

Kimiko Murakami made the soup and walked the dogs and listened and reflected and
did all the things the best sister ever does. I am forever grateful for my bessie b'zoo.

Judah Murakami made me laugh, hugged me when I didn't know I needed it, and
taught me everything I needed to know about Minecraft and most everything else.
I give thanks for his little face.

My mother, Monika Murakami, moved to Toronto when I began to write this book,
and brought her gentle heart with her. I give thanks for having our whole strange
family here in this strange place.

Juniper listened thoughtfully as I recited these poems to her, then curled up for a
snooze. I give thanks for my old, wheezy dog.

Maddy and Ross Macnab came into the picture with their wit and warmth, and let me
win at Catan. Thanks, you two.

To my dear second family, of whom Heather Curley, Brock Hessel, Teri Horowitz,
Jade LaMarche, Jessica Lineham, and Krista Mennell are no small branch: for walking
with me on the path, for late-night sushi, group texts, and endless, life-giving hugs:
gratitude, always.

Tim Macnab brought tea and tidy and gave me daily, compelling reasons to come back
to the here and now. Thank you, my love.

SACHIKO MURAKAMI

is the author of two previous poetry collections with Talonbooks, *The Invisibility Exhibit* (2008), a finalist for the Governor General's Literary Award and the Gerald Lampert Memorial Award, and *Rebuild* (2011). She is the creator of the online poetry projects Project Rebuild (*projectrebuild.ca*), HENKO (*powellstreethenko.ca*), WIHTBOAM (*whenihavethebodyofaman.com*), and co-creator of FIGURE (*figureoracle.com*), an online poetry oracle, with Angela Rawlings. Murakami holds an MA in English Literature and Creative Writing from Concordia University (2006). She has been a literary worker for various Canadian presses, journals, and organizations, and sits on the poetry board at Talonbooks. Her website is *sachikomurakami.com*.